All About

PARIS

★ A Kid's Travel Guide to the Big City! ★

TABLE OF CONTENTS

WELCOME TO PARIS   2

NEIGHBORHOODS   7

GETTING AROUND   20

FAMOUS LANDMARKS   27

MUSEUMS   37

PARKS & GARDENS   43

ENTERTAINMENT & ACTIVITIES 50

SPORTS & RECREATION   54

FOOD   56

SHOPPING   60

DAY TRIPS FROM PARIS   62

USEFUL INFORMATION   66

Welcome to Paris!

Welcome to the magical city of Paris! Paris is the capital city of France and is located in the heart of Europe. It is famous for its beautiful landmarks, delicious food, and rich culture.

Paris has a long and fascinating history that spans over 2,000 years. The city was founded by a Celtic people called the Parisii in the 3rd century BC. In the Middle Ages, Paris became the capital of France and grew into a powerful city with a thriving economy. During the 18th century, Paris was a center of art and culture, and it played a crucial role in the French Revolution, which saw the

★

Paris is also known as the "City of Light" because it was one of the first cities in the world to have street lighting.

overthrow of the monarchy and the establishment of a republic. In the 19th century, Paris became a beacon of creativity and inspiration for artists, writers, and intellectuals from around the world. It was during this time that many of the city's famous landmarks, such as the Eiffel Tower and the Louvre Museum, were built.

Today, Paris is a bustling and vibrant city that continues to attract millions of visitors each year. From the Champs-Elysées to the River Seine, there is so much to see and do in this amazing city. Let's explore all the wonders that Paris has to offer!

Let's Go!

Write about what you're excited to see on your trip.

_____

_____

_____

_____

_____

Packing List

Make a list of all the things you need for your trip.

☐ _____   ☐ _____

☐ _____   ☐ _____

☐ _____   ☐ _____

☐ _____   ☐ _____

☐ _____   ☐ _____

Scavenger Hunt

Check off all the things you see in during your trip!

☐ Eiffel Tower

☐ Croissant

☐ Flag of France

☐ Café

☐ Gold statue

☐ Louvre Pyramid

☐ Pigeons

☐ Scooter

☐ Metro Sign

☐ Baguette

Paris Map

A map of Paris is an essential tool for navigating the city! The Seine River divides the city in half, with the Left Bank and Right Bank. Most of the famous monuments, such as the Eiffel Tower and the Arc de Triomphe, are located on the Right Bank. Understanding the geography of Paris can help you plan your itinerary and navigate the city more easily!

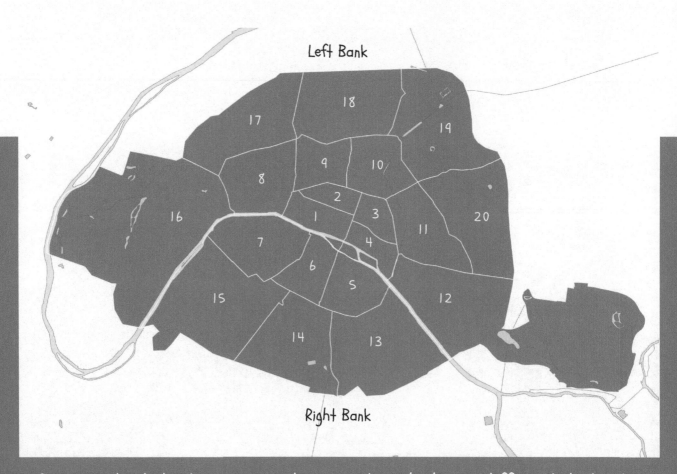

Paris is divided into 20 arrondissements, which are different districts. Each arrondissement has its own unique character and landmarks

Neighborhoods

Paris is a city with many different neighborhoods, each with its own unique charm. Here are some popular neighborhoods around Paris.

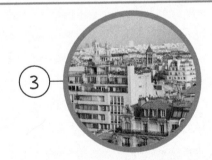

① MONTMARTRE

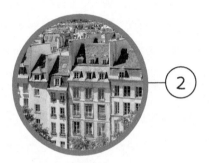

② THE MARAIS

③ SAINT-GERMAIN-DES-PRÉS

④ LATIN QUARTER

⑤ MONTPARNASSE

⑥ BELLEVILLE

Montmartre

The Montmartre neighborhood is located on a hill and is famous for its stunning views of the city. It's home to the famous Sacré-Cœur Basilica. Montmartre is also known for its street artists and performers, who create a fun and bohemian place for visitors.

The Moulin Rouge, a famous cabaret, was the birthplace of the modern cancan dance.

Montmartre was once a rural village outside of Paris. It became a popular destination for artists and writers in the late 19th and early 20th centuries, including Pablo Picasso, Vincent van Gogh, and Ernest Hemingway.

9

The Marais

The Marais neighborhood is full of narrow, winding streets that are perfect for exploring on foot. The Marais is known for its beautiful architecture, art galleries, and trendy boutiques.

The Place des Vosges, a public square in the Marais, was built in the early 17th century. It's considered one of the most beautiful squares in Paris

★

Many of the buildings
in the Marais date
back to the 17th and
18th centuries and
have a distinct style.

Saint-Germain-des-Prés

Saint-Germain-des-Prés is located on the left bank of the Seine River. It's famous for its bookstores and cafés like the Café de Flore. It's a great area to soak up the atmosphere of Parisian life and to try some delicious French pastries.

The Saint-Germain-des-Prés Church is the oldest church in Paris. It dates back to the 6th century.

13

Latin Quarter

The Latin Quarter is also located on the left bank of the Seine River and is home to many famous landmarks, including the Sorbonne University and the Pantheon. The Latin Quarter is also known for its many cafés and restaurants, as well as its lively nightlife.

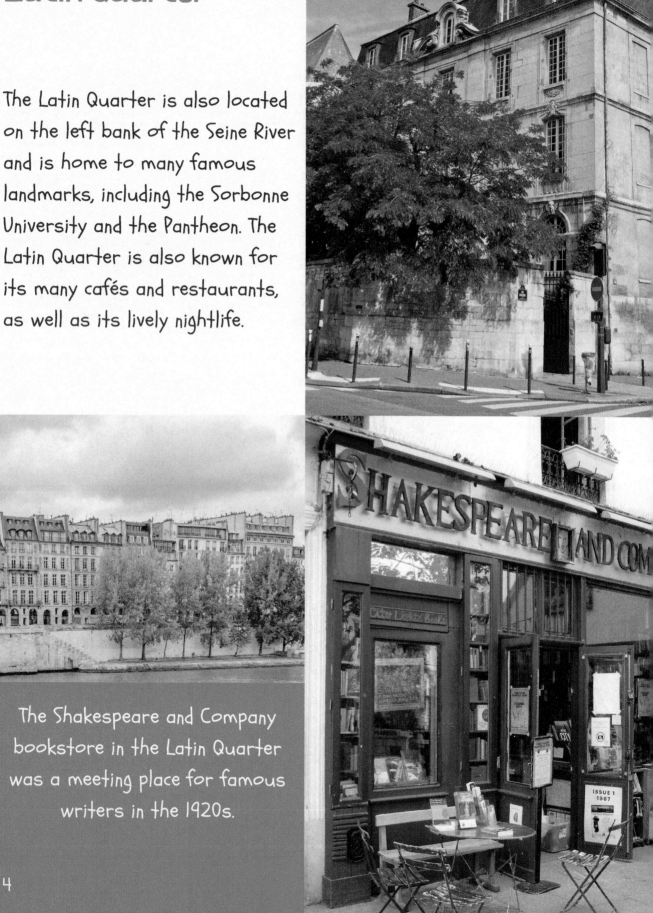

The Shakespeare and Company bookstore in the Latin Quarter was a meeting place for famous writers in the 1920s.

SORBONNE

The Sorbonne is one of the oldest universities in Europe dating back to the 12th century. Today, it's one of the largest universities in France.

Montparnasse

This neighborhood is located in the heart of Paris and is a great place to go shopping. There are many street performers and musicians in the area, which add to the lively atmosphere. It's also home to the Catacombs of Paris, an underground maze of human bones!

THE MONTPARNASSE TOWER IS THE TALLEST SKYSCRAPER IN PARIS!

17

Belleville

This neighborhood is located in West Paris and is known for its multicultural atmosphere. It's a great place to go if you want to try some different foods, as there are many ethnic restaurants in the area. Belleville is also known for its street art, which is colorful and vibrant.

Belleville Park was built in 1988 over the hilltops of the neighborhood. You can see great views of the city from here.

Getting Around

There are many ways to get around Paris! Let's explore some of the different transportation options.

① METRO

② BUS

③ TAXI

④ BOAT

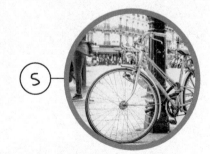

⑤ BIKE

⑥ WALKING

Metro

The metro is an underground train system that is fast and efficient. There are 16 different metro lines, and they can take you to almost any part of the city. You can buy tickets at the metro station, and there are also multi-day passes available if you plan on using the metro a lot.

Bus

Buses in Paris are safe and reliable, and they can take you to many different parts of the city. You can buy tickets at the bus stop or on the bus itself, and there are many different types of tickets to choose from, depending on how long you want to use the bus.

Taxi

If you want to travel in style, you can take a taxi. Taxis in Paris are plentiful, but they can be expensive. Make sure to agree on the price with the driver before you get in the taxi to avoid any surprises.

Boat

If you want to see the city from a different perspective, you can take a boat tour. There are many companies that offer boat tours on the River Seine, and you can see all the famous landmarks from the water. Some boats even have restaurants on board!

Bike

For a more eco-friendly option, you can rent a bike. Paris has many bike rental stations throughout the city, and it's a fun way to explore the city and get some exercise at the same time.

Walking

Finally, don't forget that walking is also a great way to see the city. Paris is a very walkable city, and there are many beautiful parks, gardens, and neighborhoods to explore on foot. Just make sure to wear comfortable shoes!

Famous Landmarks

There are many famous landmarks in Paris that you will find exciting and fascinating! Let's explore some of them together.

① EIFFEL TOWER

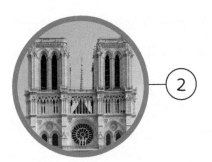

② NOTRE DAME CATHEDRAL

③ ARC DE TRIOMPHE

④ GRAND PALAIS & PETIT PALAIS

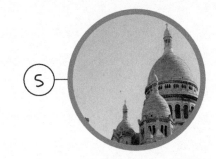

⑤ SACRÉ-CŒUR BASILICA

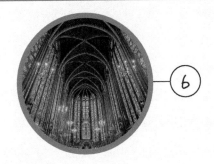

⑥ SAINT-CHAPELLE

Eiffel Tower

The Eiffel Tower is a famous landmark that represents the city's history, culture, and architecture. It's a great place to learn about engineering and technology, and offers amazing views of the city that you will never forget.

YOU CAN GET A GOOD VIEW OF THE TOWER FROM THE TROCADERO!

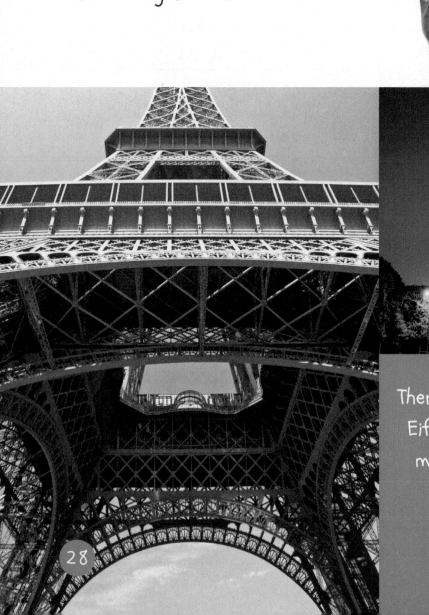

There are 20,000 light bulbs on the Eiffel Tower that twinkle for five minutes every hour after dark.

The Eiffel Tower was built for the 1889 World's Fair and was only meant to be temporary. It was so popular, they kept it.

Notre Dame Cathedral

Although it was damaged in a fire in 2019, Notre-Dame Cathedral is still a famous landmark and a beautiful example of Gothic architecture. You can explore the cathedral and learn about its history and importance to France.

The gargoyles on the cathedral play a special role in protecting the walls from water damage.

Notre Dame Cathedral is UNESCO heritage site that dates back to the 12th century and sees over 12 million visitors a year.

Arc de Triomphe

This famous monument is located at the western end of the Champs-Élysées and is a great place to take in the view of the city. You'll love climbing to the top of the monument and seeing the many streets that radiate out from it.

THE ARC DE TRIOMPHE WAS COMMISSIONED BY EMPORER NAPOLEON BONAPARTE6

Grand Palais & Petit Palais

The Grand Palais and the Petit Palais are two beautiful buildings in Paris that were built for the World's Fair in 1900. The Grand Palais is famous for its glass roof and hosts art exhibits, while the Petit Palais has a beautiful garden and an art museum inside.

THE PETIT PALAIS HOLDS OVER 1,300 ARTWORKS INSIDE ITS MUSEUM

The Grand Palais is known for its glass roof, which is made up of thousands of pieces of glass.

Sacré-Cœur Basilica

This beautiful church is located on top of a hill in the Montmartre neighborhood. Its stunning architecture includes its distinctive domes and intricate carvings. You can climb the stairs to the top of the hill and see the breathtaking views of the city!

Sainte-Chapelle

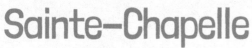

This stunning Gothic chapel is located near the Notre Dame Cathedral. Sainte-Chapelle is famous for its stained glass windows. You can see all the the beautiful colors of the windows when the light shines through the glass!

36

Museums

Paris is home to some of the world's best museums. Here are some popular museums and cultural institutions in the city!

 ①

LOUVRE MUSEUM

 ②

MUSÉE D'ORSAY

③

CENTRE POMPIDOU

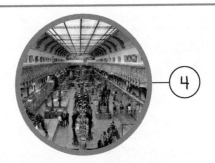 ④

NATIONAL MUSEUM OF NATURAL HISTORY

⑤

CITÉ DES SCIENCES ET DE L'INDUSTRIE

 ⑥

QUAI BRANLY MUSEUM

Louvre Museum

The Louvre is a popular museum that's home to many famous works of art, including the Mona Lisa, Venus de Milo, and Winged Victory of Samothrace. You can explore the many galleries and see all the different works of art spanning centuries.

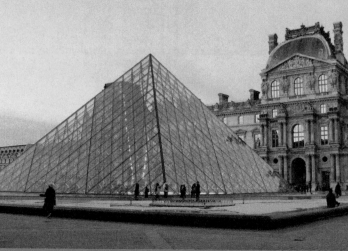

The Louvre Museum is so big, it would take you 200 days to see all 35,000 works of art!

38

Musée d'Orsay

This famous museum is home to many works of art from the 19th and 20th centuries, including works by Monet, Van Gogh, and Renoir. There are many different galleries to walk through and see all the incredible art!

Centre Pompidou

This museum is home to an impressive collection of modern and contemporary art, including works by Picasso, Matisse, and Warhol. The building itself is a work of art, with its unique inside-out design and colorful pipes on the outside.

National Museum of Natural History

The National Museum of Natural History is home to many different collections, including specimens of plants, animals, and minerals. You'll see all the many different animals, including dinosaurs, that are on display.

Cité des Sciences et de l'Industrie

The Cité des Sciences et de l'Industrie is a large science museum located in Villette Park. It's filled with interactive exhibits that teach you all about science and technology.

Quai Branly Museum

The Quai Branly Museum in Paris is dedicated to non-European art and culture. With its stunning collections of art, artifacts, and historical objects from Africa, Asia, Oceania, and the Americas, you can learn about different cultures and traditions from around the world.

Parks & Gardens

Paris is home to some of the world's most beautiful parks and gardens, providing a peaceful escape from the city. Here are a some popular parks and gardens around Paris.

① LUXEMBOURG GARDENS

② TUILERIES GARDEN

③ BUTTES-CHAUMONT PARK

④ BOIS DE VINCENNES

⑤ VILLETTE PARK

⑥ MONCEAU PARK

Luxembourg Gardens

Luxembourg Gardens is a popular park located in the Latin Quarter and is known for its beautiful gardens and large pond. You can sail boats, play on the playground, and enjoy the many statues and fountains throughout the park.

THERE ARE STATUES OF 20 FRENCH QUEENS THROUGHOUT THE GARDENS

Tuileries Garden

This large park is located in the heart of Paris and is home to many beautiful sculptures and fountains. You can ride the carousel, rent a boat to sail in the pond, or play on the playground. It's next to the Louvre Museum, so take a visit to the park after seeing the Mona Lisa.

Buttes-Chaumont Park

This huge park is home to a beautiful lake, waterfalls, and a large suspension bridge. You will love exploring the park and playing on the many different play structures. You can even climb to the top of the hill in the park to get a great view of Paris!

Bois de Vincennes

Bois de Vincennes is a park located on the outskirts of Paris and is home to many different activities, including a zoo, a lake, and a mini-golf course. There's plenty of activities to enjoy at this park. You can even bring a picnic basket and have lunch here!

47

Villette Park

Villette Park is located in the northeast of Paris. It's home to many different attractions, including a science museum, a concert hall, and a large playground.

Monceau Park

This beautiful park is known for its many statues and monuments. You can play on the playground and explore the many different areas of the park, including the pretty gardens and ponds.

Pop Quiz

1. Which river runs through Paris?
    A. Seine
    B. Thames
    C. Danube
    D. Nile

2. What is the name of the art museum in Paris that houses the Mona Lisa?
    A. Musée d'Orsay
    B. Louvre Museum
    C. Centre Pompidou
    D. Musée Rodin

3. Which historic cathedral in Paris was severely damaged in a fire in 2019?
    A. Notre Dame Cathedral
    B. Saint Paul's Cathedral
    C. St. Peter's Basilica
    D. Westminster Abbey

4. Which famous tower is an important symbol of Paris?
    A. Empire State Building
    B. Tokyo Tower
    C. Eiffel Tower
    D. Montparnasse Tower

5. In which neighborhood is the Moulin Rouge located?
    A. Saint-Germain-des-Prés
    B. Belleville
    C. Marais
    D. Montmartre

6. What is the name of the underground rail system in Paris?
    A. Subway
    B. Tube
    C. Metro
    D. Monorail

Entertainment & Activities

Paris is a vibrant place with endless entertainment and activities from sightseeing tours to festivals and events!

① SIGHTSEEING TOURS

② CLASSES

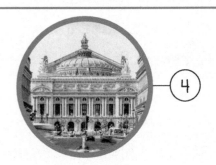

③ ZOOS & AQUARIUMS

④ SHOWS

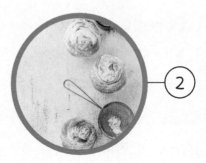

⑤ FESTIVALS & EVENTS

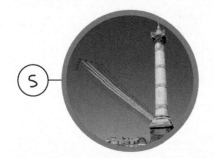

⑥ PUBLIC SQUARES

Sightseeing Tours

Paris has many fun and educational tours. Some popular options include bike tours, boat tours on the Seine, and walking tours of neighborhoods like Montmartre or the Latin Quarter.

Classes

If you're interested in learning a new skill or trying something new, there are many classes available in Paris. From cooking classes to art classes, language classes to dance classes, there are options for every interest.

Zoos & Aquariums

Paris has several zoos and aquariums where kids can see a variety of animals up close. The Paris Zoological Park, the Jardin des Plantes, and the Aquarium de Paris are all popular options.

Shows

Paris is home to many theaters and venues that offer family-friendly shows and performances. The Opéra Bastille, the Théâtre des Champs-Elysées, and the Cirque d'Hiver are just a few examples.

Festivals & Events

Paris has a lively events calendar with many festivals and events. Some popular options include the Paris Carnival in February, the Fête de la Musique in June, and the Christmas markets in December. Don't miss all the fireworks and air shows in July for Bastille Day!

Public Squares

Paris is known for its beautiful squares, many of which have playgrounds, fountains, and other fun features for kids. The Place des Vosges, the Place de la Concorde, and the Jardin du Luxembourg are just a few examples.

Sports & Recreation

Soccer

Soccer is the most popular sport in France, and there are many parks and public spaces where children can play a game. They can join in with locals or start their own game with other kids.

Tennis

Paris is the host of the famous French Open tennis tournament, but you can also play the sport at local clubs and parks.

Ice Skating

During the winter months, there are several outdoor ice skating rinks in Paris, including one at the Eiffel Tower. You can rent skates and enjoy gliding across the ice.

Skateboarding

Paris has several skate parks that are perfect for skateboarders of all levels. Kids can bring their own board or rent one from a local skate shop.

Food

Paris is famous for its diverse and delicious food scene, with some of the most iconic and tasty treats in the world.

Croissant

Croissants are a classic French pastry that is buttery and flaky. They are perfect for breakfast or a snack, and you can enjoy their light and crispy texture.

Crêpes

Crêpes are thin pancakes that can be filled with a variety of sweet or savory ingredients. You can try Nutella and banana or ham and cheese crêpes, among many other options.

Macarons

Macarons are colorful French cookies that are made with almond flour and filled with a creamy filling. They come in many different flavors, and you will love their sweet and chewy texture.

Baguettes

Baguettes are long, thin loaves
of bread that are a staple of
French cuisine. They are perfect
for making sandwiches or
enjoying with butter and jam.

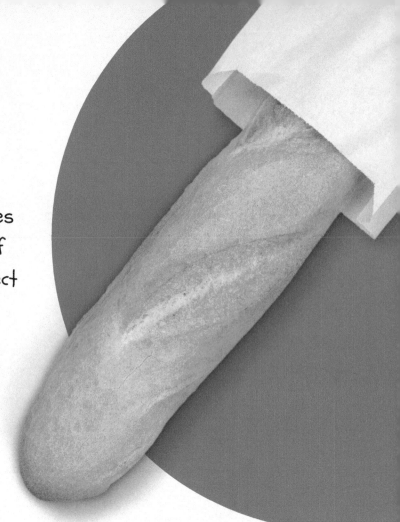

Croque-monsieur

Croque-monsieur is a classic
French sandwich made with ham
and cheese. It is typically served
warm and toasted, and it as a
gooey, melted cheese and savory
flavor.

Hot Chocolate

Paris is famous for its rich and creamy hot chocolate, which is made with melted chocolate and milk. This is the perfect indulgent treat, especially on a chilly day. You can get a hot chocolate at the famous cafe Angelina's.

Paris Laughs

- What can you find a lot of in a dumpster behind a Paris McDonald's? French Flies

- Why couldn't the family go to the Louvre? Because they didn't have the Monet to get Degas to make the Van Gogh!

- Why did the baker move to Paris? Because he wanted to make some dough!

- Why did the French person wear only stripes to the zoo? He wanted to blend in with the zebras.

Shopping

Paris is a great place to go shopping, with something for everyone. Here are some shopping destinations that are sure to delight shoppers.

Champs-Elysées

Galerie Vivienne

The Champs-Elysées is a tree-lined avenue famous for its luxury boutiques and stores, with a wide range of options for high-end shopping.

Galerie Vivienne is a covered shopping arcade built in the 19th century, popular for its upscale boutiques and artisanal shops. It's a charming shopping experience!

Department Stores

Paris has several large department stores, including the iconic Galeries Lafayette, Le Bon Marche, and Printemps. Some of these department stores have been open since the 1800s.

Markets

Paris is know for having many markets. The Marché Bastille is one of the largest, selling everything from fresh produce to antiques. The Marché aux Puces de Saint-Ouen is another popular market, selling vintage clothing, furniture, and other unique finds.

Day Trips from Paris

There are plenty of exciting day trips to take from Paris. Let's escape the city and explore more of what France has to offer!

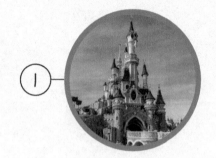

① DISNEYLAND PARIS

② PALACE OF VERSAILLES

③ PARC ASTÉRIX

④ GIVERNY

⑤ FONTAINEBLEAU

⑥ CHÂTEAU DE CHANTILLY

Disneyland Paris

Disneyland Paris is a popular theme park that offers a magical experience for kids of all ages. It has a variety of rides, shows, and attractions, and you can meet all your favorite Disney characters.

Palace of Versailles

The Palace of Versailles is a magnificent palace located just outside of Paris. You can explore the palace's ornate rooms and gardens and learn about French history.

Parc Astérix

Parc Astérix is a theme park based on the popular French comic book series, Astérix. It has a variety of rides and attractions that are themed around the characters and stories from the books.

Giverny

Giverny is a charming village that was the home of the famous French impressionist painter, Claude Monet. You can visit Monet's house and gardens and see the water lilies and other flowers that inspired his paintings.

Fontainebleau

Fontainebleau is a historic town located just outside of Paris that is known for its beautiful forest and castle. You can explore the castle's grand halls and see the horses that are trained in the forest.

Château de Chantilly

The Château de Chantilly is a beautiful castle located just outside of Paris. It has a large collection of art and artifacts, as well as beautiful gardens and a horse museum.

Useful Information

Etiquette

Souvenirs

When visiting Paris, it's important to be polite and remember basic French phrases like "Bonjour" and "Merci." In museums and historic sites, respect the exhibits and do not touch them.

Paris is a great place to find unique souvenirs such as macarons, perfume, and fashion items. Souvenir shops can be found all over the city, especially in tourist areas.

Money

The currency in France is the Euro. Be sure to have some cash on hand for small purchases, and use a credit card for larger purchases.

Language

French is the main language spoken in Paris, so it's helpful to know some basic French phrases. However, many Parisians also speak English, so don't be afraid to ask for help if you need it.

Safety

Paris is generally a safe city, but it's important to be aware of your surroundings and take precautions like keeping an eye on your belongings and avoiding unfamiliar areas at night.

Weather

Paris has a temperate climate with mild summers and cool winters. Be sure to check the weather forecast before your trip and pack appropriate clothing.

Journey's End

Write about what you enjoyed on your trip Paris.

_____

_____

_____

_____

_____

_____

_____

_____

_____

_____

Credits

Printed in Great Britain
by Amazon

40887894R00044